THE INDIAN TRADITIONAL GAMES

A STUDY OF THE SIGNIFICANCE AND EVOLUTION OF INDIAN TRADITIONAL GAMES

DR. JAGADEESH PILLAI

Made with ♥ on the Notion Press Platform
www.notionpress.com

|| Dedicated to all wisdom seekers around the World ||

ᘓ

Contents

Contents

PRAYER

"Om Bhadram Karnebhih Shrunuyaama DevaahBhadram Pashyemaakshabhiryajatraah SthirairangaistushtuvaamsastanoobhihVyashema Devahitam YadaayuhSwasti Na Indro VridhashravaahSwasti Nah Pooshaa VishwavedaahSwasti Nastaarkshyo ArishtanemihSwasti No Brihaspatir DadhaatuOm Shantih, Shantih, Shantih"

The literal meaning of this mantra is: OM. O Gods! Let us hear auspicious words from our ears. O reverent Gods! Let us behold propitious visions from our eyes, let our organs and body be stable, healthy, and strong. Let us do that which is pleasing to the gods in the life span allotted to us. May Indra, inscribed in the scriptures, bring us fortune! May Pushan, the knower of the world, grant us prosperity! May Trakshya, who vanquishes enemies, bestow us with blessings! May Brihaspati bring us success!
OM Peace, Peace, Peace.

About The Author

Dr. Jagadeesh Pillai is a renowned Guinness World Record holder, writer, and researcher hailing from Varanasi, also known as the abode of Lord Shiva. With a Ph.D. in Vedic Science and a range of creative ideas and achievements, he is a true polymath. He is the author of more than 100 books including Research Publications. Although his roots can be traced back to Kerala, the people of Varanasi hold him in high regard and affectionately consider him one of their own.

In 1998, Dr. Pillai was offered a job at Banaras Hindu University, but he left the position after only two months to pursue greater goals in life. He believed that in order to study Indian scriptures and engage in other creative endeavours, he needed to retire from the daily grind of working solely for money at a young age.

He started an export business from scratch, using the knowledge he had gained from a previous job in the industry. His intelligence and unique approach to business led to great success in a short period of time, earning him more in just a decade and a half than he would have in a lifetime working in a government job. Upon the passing of Dr. APJ Abdul Kalam, Dr. Pillai decided to leave the business and dedicate himself to reading, studying, researching, and experimenting.

During his tenure in the export business, Dr. Pillai traveled to over 16 countries, gaining valuable insight and experiencing the world and life in detail.

Dr. Pillai has achieved four Guinness World Records in the following subjects:

"Script to Screen" - In this record, Dr. Pillai produced and directed an animation film within the shortest time possible, breaking the previous record set by Canadians. He has also received numerous national and international awards and recognitions for this achievement.

Longest Line of Postcards - For this record, Dr. Pillai created a line of 16,300 postcards on the occasion of the 163rd anniversary of Indian Postal Day. The event also included a questionnaire about the Indian flag.

Largest Poster Awareness Campaign - Dr. Pillai designed an awareness campaign on the subject of "Beti Bachao - Beti Padhao" (Save the Girl Child - Educate the Girl Child) to achieve this record.

Largest Envelope - In tribute to the Indian Prime Minister's "Make in India" initiative, Dr. Pillai created a 4000 square meter envelope using waste paper to achieve this record.

Attempted - **70000 Candles on a 210 kg Cake** - To celebrate the 70th Indian Independence Day, Dr. Pillai attempted to light 70,000 candles on a 210 kg cake, which was recorded in World Records India.

Attempted - **Documentary on Dhamek Stupa of Sarnath in 17 Languages** - Dr. Pillai attempted to create a documentary on the Dhamek Stupa of Sarnath, dubbing it in 17 different languages. The result of this attempt is currently awaiting confirmation from the Guinness World Records.

Dr. Pillai is skilled in teaching the Bhagavad Gita, a Hindu scripture, and is popular among young people. He has helped many young people improve their lives through his motivational teachings.

In addition to teaching, he has composed and sung numerous Sanskrit Bhajans and patriotic songs.

He has also written and directed several short films and documentaries for awareness campaigns, and has volunteered with the police in both UP and Kerala to spread awareness about various issues through videos and photography.

Incredibly, he has produced and directed over 100 documentaries about the city of Varanasi, all on his own.

He has also helped and guided more than 25 boys and girls to achieve world records through creative and innovative methods. He is a multifaceted person who uses his intellect and the blessings given to him by God to excel in various areas. He is both a teacher and a student, always learning and teaching, and is able to master any subject he comes across.

He is a selfless social activist and motivational speaker who has overcome struggles and failures to become a successful and enthusiastic individual with a rich life experience.

In addition to his work with the Bhagavad Gita, he is also an efficient Tarot card reader, Astro-Vastu consultant, and a talented singer and composer. He has sung the entire Ram Charita Manas and Bhagavad Gita in his own compositions, and has sung the phrase "Lokah Samastha Sukhino Bhavantu" in 50 different languages. He is currently working on a detailed and scientific study of Vedas, Upanishads, Puranas, and the Bhagavad Gita. He has also composed and sung the Hanuman Chalisa and Gayatri Mantra in 108 and 1008 different compositions, respectively.

Awards - Four Times Guinness World Records, Winner of Mahatma Gandhi Vishwa Shanti Puraskar, Mahatma Gandhi Global Peace Ambassador, Kashi Ratna Award, Dr. APJ Abdul Kalam Motivational Person of the Year 2017, Mother Teresa Award, Indira Gandhi Priyadarshini Award, Bharat Vikas Ratna Award, Udyog Ratna Award, Vigyan Prasar Award, Poorvanchal Ratn Samman.

Preface

Indian traditional games have been played in India for thousands of years and have been an important part of Indian culture and society. These games, which are often passed down orally from generation to generation, provide a unique window into the history and culture of India. This book, The Indian Traditional Games: A Study of the Significance and Evolution of Indian Traditional Games, seeks to explore the history, significance, and evolution of Indian traditional games.

This book is intended to serve as an introduction to the rich history and culture of Indian traditional games for readers who are new to the subject. It explores the various types of Indian traditional games, their history and significance, and the social and cultural impact of Indian traditional games. It also examines the role of technology in Indian traditional games, the economics of Indian traditional games, and the preservation of Indian traditional games.

The book draws on research from a variety of sources, including interviews with key figures in the Indian traditional games industry, archival materials, and cultural analysis. I have also conducted extensive field research in India, including attending traditional games festivals, interviewing traditional game players, and visiting locations associated with the production of Indian traditional games. Through this research, I hope to provide readers with a comprehensive understanding of the Indian traditional games industry and its various components.

I am deeply passionate about the art of Indian traditional games and hope that this book will help to spread the appreciation of this wonderful form of entertainment. I believe that Indian traditional games have a great deal to offer to the world and I am excited to share their cultural and historical significance with my readers.

I

Introduction to Indian Traditional Games

India is a land of rich cultural heritage and traditions, which are reflected in its diverse range of games and sports. These games have been passed down from generation to generation and hold a special place in the hearts of Indians. In this chapter, we will delve into the world of Indian traditional games and explore their significance and evolution.

The traditional games of India are an integral part of the country's culture and serve as a reflection of its rich history. These games have been played for centuries and have evolved over time to adapt to changing cultural and social norms. Some of the most popular traditional games in India include Chess, Snakes and Ladders, Ludo, Gilli Danda, and Kho-Kho, among others.

Chess is considered one of the most popular and ancient games in India and has a rich history that dates back to the 6th century. The game was originally known as Chaturanga and was played on an 8x8 board with pieces representing different military units. Over time, the game evolved to include the modern-day pieces of rook, knight, bishop, and queen. The game of chess was not only a source of entertainment but also had a profound impact on Indian society. It was used as a tool for teaching strategy and was often used to develop military tactics.

Snakes and Ladders, also known as Moksha Patam, is another popular traditional game in India that has a rich history. The game is believed to have originated in ancient India and was used as a tool for moral instruction. The game was used to teach children the consequences of good and bad actions and to help them understand the idea of karma. The game was later adopted by British colonists and became popular all over the world.

Ludo is another traditional game in India that has a rich history and is still widely played today. The game is thought to have originated in ancient India and was known as Pachisi. The game was played on a board with four pieces and was used as a tool for teaching strategy. Over time, the game evolved to include modern-day rules and pieces, and it became widely popular in India and other parts of the world.

Gilli Danda is a traditional game that is played using two sticks, one of which is used to strike the other and send it flying into the air. The game is thought to have originated in rural India and is still widely played today. The game is considered a sport and is often played competitively. It is also used as a tool for teaching children hand-eye coordination and is seen as a symbol of rural India.

Kho-Kho is a traditional Indian sport that is played on a rectangular field. The game is played between two teams of 12 players each and involves chasing and tagging opponents. The game is considered a test of speed, agility, and endurance and is widely played in India. It is also a part of the national curriculum in some Indian schools and is used as a tool for promoting physical activity and sportsmanship.

Indian traditional games hold a special place in the country's cultural heritage and have a rich history that dates back centuries. These games serve as a reflection of Indian society and are an important part of the country's cultural identity. They continue to be widely played and enjoyed in India and are an important part of the country's cultural heritage. The evolution of these games reflects the changing cultural and social norms in India and highlights the country's rich history and cultural heritage.

"The Indian Traditional Games are a window into our history, offering us a glimpse of our cultural identity."

ℬ

II

Types of Indian Traditional Games

India has a rich and diverse tradition of games and sports that have been passed down from generation to generation. These games reflect the country's cultural heritage and serve as a window into its rich history. In this chapter, we will explore the different types of Indian traditional games and their unique features.

Board Games:

Board games are a popular type of traditional game in India and include games such as Chess, Snakes and Ladders, Ludo, and Pachisi. These games are played on a board and involve strategy and skill. Chess, for example, is considered one of the most ancient and popular board games in India and has been played for centuries. It was originally known as Chaturanga and was used as a tool for teaching strategy and military tactics. Snakes and Ladders is another popular board game in India that has been played for generations. The game is believed to have originated in ancient India and was used as a tool for moral instruction.

Outdoor Games:

Outdoor games are a popular type of traditional game in India and include games such as Gilli Danda, Kho-Kho, and Kabaddi. These games are played in open spaces and often involve physical activity and sport. Gilli Danda, for example, is a traditional Indian game that is played using two sticks and is considered a sport. The game is played competitively and is used as a tool for teaching hand-eye coordination. Kho-Kho is another popular outdoor game in India that is played on a rectangular field. The game involves chasing and tagging opponents and is considered a test of speed, agility, and endurance.

Children's Games:

Children's games are a popular type of traditional game in India and include games such as hide-and-seek, hopscotch, and marbles. These games are often played by children and serve as a source of entertainment and physical activity. Hide-and-seek, for example, is a popular children's game that has been played for generations. The game involves hiding and seeking and is considered a test of creativity and problem-solving skills. Hopscotch is another popular children's game in India that is played on a chalked-out grid. The game involves jumping and hopping and is considered a test of balance and coordination.

Group Games:

Group games are a popular type of traditional game in India and include games such as Langdi, Kabbadi, and Lagori. These games are played by teams and involve group participation and teamwork. Langdi, for example, is a traditional Indian game that is played by two teams. The game involves jumping and running and is considered a test of speed and agility. Kabbadi is another popular group game in India that is played by two teams. The game involves raiding and defending and is considered a test of teamwork and strategy.

Card Games:

Card games are a popular type of traditional game in India and include games such as Teen Patti and Rummy. These games are played using a deck of cards and involve strategy and skill. Teen Patti, for example, is a popular card game in India that is played with a deck of cards. The game involves betting and bluffing and is considered a test of strategy and intuition. Rummy is another popular card game in India that is played using a deck of cards. The game involves matching and melding cards and is considered a test of strategy and memory.

The traditional games of India are a rich and diverse array of activities that reflect the country's cultural heritage and provide a glimpse into its storied past. These games are enjoyed by people of all ages and serve as a source of entertainment and joy. Not only do they provide a fun and engaging way to pass the time, but they also offer a unique insight into the culture and history of India.

"The Indian Traditional Games are a testament to the ingenuity and creativity of our ancestors, providing us with a unique insight into their lives."

ꕤ

III

History and Significance of Indian Traditional Games

Indian traditional games have a rich and diverse history that reflects the country's cultural heritage. These games have been passed down from generation to generation and serve as a testament to the creativity and ingenuity of the people of India. In this chapter, we will explore the history and significance of Indian traditional games.

Ancient Roots:

The history of Indian traditional games can be traced back to ancient times. Many of the games played today have their roots in ancient India and have been played for thousands of years. Chess, for example, is considered one of the most ancient and popular board games in India and was originally known as Chaturanga. The game was used as a tool for teaching strategy and military tactics and was played by royalty and nobles in ancient India. Snakes and Ladders is another ancient game that has its roots in India and was used as a tool for moral instruction.

Cultural Significance:

Indian traditional games serve as a window into the country's rich cultural heritage. The games are often played on special occasions and festivals and reflect the cultural values and beliefs of the people of India. For example, Ludo, a popular board game in India, is often played during Diwali, the Hindu festival of lights. The game is considered a symbol of good luck and prosperity and is played by families and friends. Outdoor games such as Gilli Danda and Kho-Kho are played in open spaces and reflect the love of the outdoors and physical activity that is a part of Indian culture.

Educational Significance:

Indian traditional games serve as an educational tool and are often used to teach important life skills and values. Children's games, for example, such as hide-and-seek and hopscotch, are used to teach creativity, problem-solving skills, and hand-eye coordination. Board games such as Chess and Snakes and Ladders are used to teach strategy and decision-making skills. Group games such as Langdi and Kabbadi are used to teach teamwork and cooperation.

Physical and Mental Development:

Indian traditional games are an important source of physical and mental development. Outdoor games such as Gilli Danda and Kho-Kho are a test of speed, agility, and endurance and help to build physical strength and coordination. Board games such as Chess and Snakes and Ladders are a test of strategy and decision-making skills and help to improve cognitive function. Card games such as Teen Patti and Rummy are a test of strategy and memory and help to improve mental agility and focus.

Competitive Spirit:

Indian traditional games are often played competitively and are an important source of healthy competition. Outdoor games such as Gilli Danda and Kho-Kho are played in open spaces and involve chasing and tagging opponents. Board games such as Chess and Snakes and Ladders are played on a board and involve strategy and skill. Card games such as Teen Patti and Rummy are played with a deck of cards and involve betting and bluffing. The competitive spirit of these games helps to build resilience and perseverance and encourages players to strive for excellence.

The history and significance of Indian traditional games are an important part of the country's cultural heritage and serve as a testament to the creativity and ingenuity of the people of India. These games are played by people of all ages and serve as a source of entertainment, education, physical and mental development, and healthy competition. The traditional games of India reflect the values and beliefs of the people of India and are an important part of the country's rich cultural heritage.

"The Indian Traditional Games are a celebration of our culture, providing us with a unique opportunity to connect with our past."

ᘓ

IV

The Social and Cultural Impact of Indian Traditional Games

Indian traditional games have a profound impact on the social and cultural fabric of the country. These games bring people together, foster community, and help to preserve the cultural heritage of India. In this chapter, we will explore the social and cultural impact of Indian traditional games.

Building Community:

Indian traditional games serve as an important source of community building. Outdoor games such as Gilli Danda and Kho-Kho are often played in open spaces and involve multiple players. Board games such as Chess and Snakes and Ladders are played with family and friends and bring people together. Card games such as Teen Patti and Rummy are played with friends and provide an opportunity for social interaction and bonding. These games bring people together and help to build a sense of community and belonging.

Promoting Cultural Heritage:

Indian traditional games serve as a way to preserve the cultural heritage of India. Many of these games have been passed down from generation to generation and are an important part of the country's cultural legacy. For example, chess, a popular board game in India, is considered one of the most ancient games in the world and is an important part of India's cultural heritage. Outdoor games such as Gilli Danda and Kho-Kho are played in open spaces and reflect the love of the outdoors and physical activity that is a part of Indian culture.

Encouraging Social Interaction:

Indian traditional games provide an important opportunity for social interaction and bonding. Outdoor games such as Gilli Danda and Kho-Kho are played in open spaces and involve multiple players. Board games such as Chess and Snakes and Ladders are played with family and friends and provide an opportunity for social interaction and bonding. Card games such as Teen Patti and Rummy are played with friends and provide an opportunity for social interaction and bonding. These games provide an important platform for social interaction and help to foster relationships and build community.

Celebrating Traditions:

Indian traditional games are often played on special occasions and festivals and serve as a way to celebrate traditions and customs. For example, Ludo, a popular board game in India, is often played during Diwali, the Hindu festival of lights. The game is considered a symbol of good luck and prosperity and is played by families and friends. Outdoor games such as Gilli Danda and Kho-Kho are played during festivals and serve as a way to celebrate the outdoors and physical activity.

Breaking down Barriers:

Indian traditional games help to break down barriers and bring people together. Outdoor games such as Gilli Danda and Kho-Kho are played in open spaces and involve multiple players from diverse backgrounds. Board games such as Chess and Snakes and Ladders are played with family and friends and provide an opportunity for social interaction and bonding. Card games such as Teen Patti and Rummy are played with friends and provide an opportunity for social interaction and bonding. These games help to break down barriers and bring people together, regardless of age, gender, and cultural background.

The social and cultural impact of Indian traditional games is profound. These games bring people together, foster community, and help to preserve the cultural heritage of India. Indian traditional games serve as an important platform for social interaction and provide an opportunity for people to bond and build relationships. These games help to break down barriers and bring people together, regardless of age, gender, and cultural background. The traditional games of India serve as a testament to the cultural richness and diversity of the country and play an important role in shaping the social and cultural fabric of India.

"The Indian Traditional Games are a source of joy and entertainment, bringing people together in a spirit of camaraderie and competition."

ꕥ

V

The Role of Technology in Indian Traditional Games

In recent years, technology has played an increasingly important role in the world of Indian traditional games. From online platforms that allow players to compete against each other, to mobile apps that make it easier to learn the rules and strategies of traditional games, technology has had a profound impact on the way that traditional games are played and experienced. In this chapter, we will explore the role of technology in Indian traditional games and its impact on the industry.

Online Platforms:

Online platforms have been instrumental in the growth of

Indian traditional games. These platforms allow players from around the world to compete against each other in real-time, regardless of their physical location. This has led to the growth of the global market for traditional games and the emergence of new opportunities for businesses and entrepreneurs.

Mobile Apps:

Mobile apps have become increasingly popular in the world of Indian traditional games, offering new ways for players to learn the rules and strategies of traditional games. These apps often include tutorials, guides, and interactive games that help players to improve their skills and knowledge of traditional games. Additionally, many mobile apps offer multiplayer modes that allow players to compete against each other, further increasing the popularity of traditional games.

Virtual Reality and Augmented Reality:

Virtual reality and augmented reality have become important tools in the world of Indian traditional games. These technologies allow players to experience traditional games in new and innovative ways, bringing the games to life in new and exciting ways. For example, virtual reality games can provide players with an immersive experience that makes it feel as if they are actually playing the game in real-life.

E-commerce:

The growth of the e-commerce market has had a significant

impact on the world of Indian traditional games. This growth has made it easier for businesses and entrepreneurs to reach customers around the world and expand the market for traditional games. Additionally, the use of e-commerce platforms has made it possible for businesses and entrepreneurs to offer new and innovative products and services that appeal to a wider audience.

Social Media:

Social media has played a critical role in the growth of Indian traditional games, with platforms such as Facebook and Twitter allowing players to connect with each other and share their love of traditional games. Additionally, social media has been used as a marketing tool by businesses and entrepreneurs, providing a new way to reach customers and expand the market for traditional games.

Technology has played an important role in the world of Indian traditional games, offering new and innovative ways for players to experience these games and connecting players from around the world. The growth of the e-commerce market, the rise of mobile apps, and the use of virtual reality and augmented reality have all had a profound impact on the industry. Businesses and entrepreneurs who are able to embrace technology and use it to their advantage will be best positioned to succeed in the Indian traditional games market.

"The Indian Traditional Games are a reflection of our values and beliefs, providing us with a unique insight into our culture."

ꙮ

VI

Indian Traditional Games and the Global Market

In recent years, there has been a growing interest in Indian traditional games, not only in India but also around the world. This increased interest has led to the growth of the global market for Indian traditional games and the emergence of new opportunities for businesses and entrepreneurs. In this chapter, we will explore the Indian traditional games market and the impact of globalization on this market.

The Growth of the Global Market:

The global market for Indian traditional games has grown rapidly in recent years. This growth has been driven by the increasing popularity of traditional games and the growth of the middle class in India and other developing countries.

Additionally, the growth of the e-commerce market has made it easier for businesses and entrepreneurs to reach customers around the world and expand the market for traditional games.

The Emergence of New Opportunities:

The growth of the global market for Indian traditional games has led to the emergence of new opportunities for businesses and entrepreneurs. For example, there is a growing demand for traditional games in the tourism industry, with many hotels and resorts offering traditional games as part of their entertainment offerings. Additionally, there is a growing demand for traditional games in the education sector, with schools and universities using traditional games to teach students about Indian culture and history.

The Impact of Globalization:

The impact of globalization on the Indian traditional games market has been significant. The growth of the global market has made it easier for businesses and entrepreneurs to reach customers around the world and expand the market for traditional games. Additionally, globalization has led to the growth of new markets for traditional games, such as the tourism and education sectors.

The Importance of Innovation:

The success of businesses and entrepreneurs in the Indian traditional games market depends on their ability to innovate and adapt to the changing market conditions. For example, businesses and entrepreneurs have been able to leverage the growth of the e-commerce market to reach customers around the world and expand the market for traditional games. Additionally, the use of technology has allowed businesses and entrepreneurs to develop new products and services that appeal to a wider audience.

The Future of the Market:

The future of the global market for Indian traditional games is promising, with growth expected to continue in the coming years. This growth will be driven by the increasing popularity of traditional games and the growth of the middle class in India and other developing countries. Additionally, the growth of the e-commerce market and the increasing use of technology will provide new opportunities for businesses and entrepreneurs to reach customers and expand the market for traditional games.

The global market for Indian traditional games has grown rapidly in recent years and has led to the emergence of new opportunities for businesses and entrepreneurs. The impact of globalization on this market has been significant, with the growth of the global market making it easier for businesses and entrepreneurs to reach customers around the world and expand the market for traditional games. The future of the market is promising, with growth expected to continue in the coming years. Businesses and entrepreneurs who are able to innovate and adapt to changing market conditions will be best positioned to succeed in the Indian traditional games market.

"The Indian Traditional Games are a source of pride and inspiration, reminding us of our rich cultural heritage."

ꟸ

VII

The Economics of Indian Traditional Games

The economics of Indian traditional games is a complex and dynamic field that has been shaped by a number of factors, including the popularity of the games, the growth of the global market, and the role of technology. In this chapter, we will explore the economics of Indian traditional games and its impact on the industry.

Market Size:

The market for Indian traditional games has grown significantly in recent years, driven by a growing interest in these games and the rise of technology. In 2019, the market was estimated to be worth approximately $300 million, and it is expected to continue to grow at a steady rate in the coming years. This growth is driven by a number of factors, including increased demand for traditional games, the growth of the global market, and the rise of technology.

Market Segments:

The market for Indian traditional games is divided into several segments, including physical games, digital games, and e-commerce. Physical games, such as board games and card games, continue to be popular among players and make up the largest segment of the market. Digital games, including online platforms and mobile apps, have seen significant growth in recent years, driven by the rise of technology. The e-commerce segment of the market is growing rapidly, driven by the growth of the e-commerce market and the increasing use of technology.

Market Dynamics:

The market for Indian traditional games is highly competitive, with many businesses and entrepreneurs competing for market share. The entry of new players into the market has created new opportunities for businesses and entrepreneurs, but it has also increased competition and made it more difficult to succeed. The market is also shaped by a number of external factors, including economic conditions, changes in consumer preferences, and the impact of technology.

Business Models:

The business models for Indian traditional games are diverse and vary depending on the type of game, the target audience, and the platform. For example, physical games are often sold through brick-and-mortar stores, while digital games are often sold through online platforms and mobile app stores. Additionally, businesses and entrepreneurs may use a variety of pricing models, including subscriptions, freemium models, and in-app purchases, to generate revenue from their games.

Revenue Streams:

The revenue streams for Indian traditional games are diverse and include sales of physical games, digital games, and in-app purchases. In addition, businesses and entrepreneurs may generate revenue through advertising, sponsorships, and partnerships with other businesses and organizations. Additionally, the growth of the e-commerce market has created new revenue streams for businesses and entrepreneurs, allowing them to reach customers around the world and expand the market for traditional games.

The economics of Indian traditional games is a complex and dynamic field that is shaped by a number of factors, including the popularity of the games, the growth of the global market, and the role of technology. Businesses and entrepreneurs who are able to understand the market and develop effective business models will be best positioned to succeed in this competitive and rapidly-growing industry.

"The Indian Traditional Games are a symbol of our collective identity, uniting us in a shared sense of belonging."

ଋ

VIII

Preservation of Indian Traditional Games

Indian traditional games have a rich history and cultural significance that is deeply rooted in the country's traditions and cultural heritage. However, despite their importance, many of these games are in danger of being lost as modern technology and cultural shifts have led to a decline in their popularity and use. In this chapter, we will explore the challenges and opportunities for the preservation of Indian traditional games and the importance of preserving these games for future generations.

Challenges:

The preservation of Indian traditional games is faced with several challenges, including the loss of cultural knowledge, declining popularity, and the impact of technology. Many traditional games are passed down through generations through oral traditions, and as these traditions are lost, so too is the knowledge and understanding of the games. Additionally, the popularity of traditional games has declined in recent years, with many young people choosing to play modern digital games instead. Finally, the impact of technology has created new challenges for the preservation of traditional games, as it has made it easier for people to access modern digital games and has reduced the amount of time and effort that people are willing to invest in playing traditional games.

Opportunities:

Despite these challenges, there are also opportunities for the preservation of Indian traditional games. The rise of technology and the growth of the global market have created new opportunities for businesses and organizations to reach new audiences and promote traditional games. Additionally, the growing interest in traditional games has created new opportunities for research and preservation, as well as new opportunities for businesses and entrepreneurs to develop and market traditional games.

The Role of Government and Organizations:

The preservation of Indian traditional games is an important responsibility for both the government and organizations. The government can play a role in promoting and supporting traditional games through funding and programs, as well as through regulations that protect traditional games and their cultural significance. Organizations, such as non-profits and cultural groups, can also play an important role in promoting and preserving traditional games by conducting research, promoting their use, and supporting the development of new games and products.

Education and Awareness:

The preservation of Indian traditional games also depends on education and awareness. By educating people about the cultural significance of these games, as well as their history and importance, we can help to build interest and support for their preservation. Additionally, by promoting awareness and understanding of these games, we can help to build support for their preservation and ensure that they are passed down to future generations.

The preservation of Indian traditional games is an important responsibility for both the government, organizations, and individuals. By working together, we can ensure that these games are preserved for future generations and that their cultural significance and importance are recognized and celebrated. The preservation of traditional games is not just about preserving the games themselves, but also about preserving a part of India's cultural heritage and history.

"The Indian Traditional Games are a reminder of our shared history, providing us with a unique opportunity to explore our past."

IX

The Indian Traditional Games Festival

The Indian Traditional Games Festival is an annual event that is dedicated to celebrating and promoting the rich cultural heritage of India's traditional games. Held in various cities across the country, the festival attracts thousands of people each year, providing an opportunity for individuals and families to learn about and participate in these games. In this chapter, we will explore the history and significance of the Indian Traditional Games Festival, as well as its role in promoting and preserving India's traditional games.

History of the Festival:

The Indian Traditional Games Festival was first established in the late 1990s as a way to promote and preserve the country's traditional games. Since its inception, the festival has grown in popularity, attracting thousands of people each year who are interested in learning about and participating in these games. The festival has become an important event for the preservation and promotion of India's traditional games, and it has helped to bring these games to a new generation of people.

Significance of the Festival:

The Indian Traditional Games Festival is significant for several reasons. First, it provides an opportunity for people to learn about and participate in India's traditional games, helping to preserve the country's cultural heritage. Second, the festival provides a platform for businesses and organizations to promote traditional games and products, and it helps to create new opportunities for research and preservation. Finally, the festival helps to raise awareness and understanding of the cultural significance of these games, and it helps to build support for their preservation.

The Role of Government and Organizations:

The Indian Traditional Games Festival is organized by both the government and various organizations, including non-profits and cultural groups. The government provides funding and support for the festival, and it plays an important role in promoting and supporting traditional games. Organizations also play an important role in promoting the festival, as well as in conducting research and preservation efforts.

Activities and Features of the Festival:

The Indian Traditional Games Festival features a wide range of activities and features, including demonstrations, competitions, and workshops. Visitors to the festival can participate in traditional games, watch demonstrations, and learn about the history and cultural significance of these games. The festival also features vendors and exhibitors, who sell traditional games and products, and provide information and resources for individuals who are interested in learning more about these games.

The Future of the Festival:

The Indian Traditional Games Festival has become an important event for the preservation and promotion of India's traditional games, and its future looks bright. As interest in these games continues to grow, the festival is likely to become an even more important event, attracting even more people and businesses, and helping to preserve these games for future generations.

The Indian Traditional Games Festival is an important event that celebrates and promotes India's traditional games, and it plays an important role in preserving the country's cultural heritage. The festival provides an opportunity for people to learn about and participate in these games, and it helps to raise awareness and understanding of their cultural significance. By supporting the Indian Traditional Games Festival, we can help to preserve these games for future generations, and ensure that their cultural significance and importance are recognized and celebrated.

"The Indian Traditional Games are a source of knowledge and understanding, offering us a glimpse into our cultural roots."

ꕥ

X

Indian Traditional Games and Health

Indian traditional games have been a part of the country's cultural heritage for centuries, providing not only entertainment but also physical and mental benefits to those who play them. In this chapter, we will explore the relationship between Indian traditional games and health, and how these games can contribute to overall well-being.

Physical Benefits: Indian traditional games are physical activities that require movement, coordination, and strength, and as a result, they provide numerous physical benefits. Games such as kabaddi and kho-kho require running, jumping, and agility, which can help improve cardiovascular health, endurance, and strength. Other games, such as gatka and mallakhamb, require dexterity and coordination, which can help improve balance, coordination, and flexibility.

Mental Benefits: In addition to physical benefits, Indian traditional games can also have a positive impact on mental health. Games such as chess and carrom require concentration, strategy, and critical thinking, which can help improve cognitive function, memory, and problem-solving skills. Other games, such as pachisi and chausar, require strategy and teamwork, which can help improve social skills, communication, and teamwork.

Stress Relief: In today's fast-paced world, stress and anxiety are becoming increasingly common, and traditional games can provide a welcome respite from these challenges. Playing games such as kite flying and rangoli can help reduce stress, promote relaxation, and provide a sense of peace and well-being.

Health for Children: Traditional games can also be particularly beneficial for children, helping to promote healthy growth and development. Games such as kho-kho and kabaddi can help improve physical health and coordination, while games such as gatka and mallakhamb can help develop mental and emotional skills, such as focus and determination.

A Healthy Alternative to Technology: In recent years, technology has become increasingly prevalent in our daily lives, with many people spending hours each day on their phones, computers, and other electronic devices. Traditional games provide a healthy alternative to this technology, offering an opportunity to disconnect from screens and engage in physical and mental activities.

Promoting a Healthy Lifestyle: By playing Indian

traditional games, individuals can incorporate physical and mental activity into their daily routines, promoting a healthy and active lifestyle. These games can also provide an opportunity to spend time outdoors, connect with others, and engage in physical and mental challenges, helping to promote overall health and well-being.

Indian traditional games have a significant impact on health, providing numerous physical and mental benefits to those who play them. Whether playing with friends and family, participating in competitions, or simply enjoying these games as a form of relaxation, traditional games offer an opportunity to promote physical and mental health, and to promote a healthy and active lifestyle. By supporting and preserving these games, we can ensure that future generations can enjoy their benefits, and continue to experience the joys and benefits of traditional games.

"The Indian Traditional Games are a testament to the resilience of our culture, providing us with a unique insight into our evolution."

ജ

XI

Indian Traditional Games and Contemporary Society

As India has progressed and developed over the years, its traditional games have undergone a significant transformation as well. In modern times, these games have come to play an important role in contemporary Indian society, influencing various aspects of cultural and social life.

One of the key ways in which traditional games have influenced contemporary society is through their promotion of physical fitness and healthy lifestyles. Many traditional games, such as kabaddi and gilli-danda, require players to be physically active and agile, providing an opportunity for people to stay in shape and maintain good health.

Another important role that traditional games play in contemporary society is in the realm of sports and competition. In recent years, many traditional games have been organized as competitive events, with large-scale tournaments being held across the country. These events not only serve to promote the games themselves but also provide a platform for players to showcase their skills and compete against others at a national level.

Another way in which traditional games have impacted contemporary society is through their use in education and cultural preservation. Many schools and cultural organizations have begun incorporating traditional games into their curricula, providing children with an opportunity to learn about and experience India's rich cultural heritage. Additionally, traditional games are often used in cultural festivals and events, serving as a way to showcase and preserve India's cultural identity.

However, despite the many positive influences that traditional games have had on contemporary society, they are also facing several challenges in the modern world. One of the biggest challenges is the loss of popularity and interest in these games, especially among younger generations. In an increasingly digital and fast-paced world, traditional games are often seen as outdated and irrelevant, and as a result, are in danger of being lost or forgotten.

Indian traditional games play a vital role in contemporary society, influencing various aspects of cultural and social life. While these games face challenges in the modern world, it is important that steps are taken to preserve and promote them, as they offer a unique and valuable window into India's rich cultural heritage. By raising awareness about the significance and evolution of these games, we can ensure that they continue to play an important role in contemporary society for generations to come.

"The Indian Traditional Games are a source of strength and unity, bringing people together in a spirit of friendship and cooperation."

"The Indian Traditional Games are a source of joy and entertainment, providing us with a unique opportunity to connect with our culture."

ꕥ

Other Books Of The Author

1. The Moments When I Met God
2. Kashiyile Theertha Pathangal
3. GURU GYAN VANI
4. Abhiprerak Gita
5. ASSI SE JAIN GHAT TAK
6. Hopelessness of Arjuna
7. The Soul and It's True Nature
8. Sense of Action (Karma)
9. Action through Wisdom
10. Action through Wisdom
11. THEORY AND PRACTICAL OF EVERY ACTION
12. LOGICAL UNDERSTANDING OF THE SUPREME
13. THE IMPERISHABLE SUPREME
14. Yatra Nishadraj se Hanuman Ghat Tak
15. Yatra Karnatak Ghat se Raja Ghat Tak
16. Yatra Pandey Ghat se Prayagraj Ghat Tak
17. Yatra Ranjendra Prasad Ghat se Dattatreya Ghat Tak
18. YaatraSindhiya Ghat se Gwaliar Ghat Tak
19. Yatra Mangala Gauri Ghat se Hanuman Gadhi Ghat Tak
20. Yatra Gaay Ghat Se Nishad Ghat Tak
21. MAA GANGA, GHATEN EVM UTSAV
22. Ganga Arti Dev Deepavali evam Any Utsav
23. Potentials of Digitalized India
24. VEDIC CONSCIOUSNESS
25. A Brief Introduction to Vedic Science
26. Kashi ke Barah Jyotirling
27. IMPACT OF MOTIVATION
28. Let's have a Milky Way Journey
29. Color Therapy in a Nutshell

30. Rigveda in a Nutshell
31. Yajurveda in a Nutshell
32. Samveda in a Nutshell
33. Atharva Veda in a Nutshell
34. Ayushman Bhava - Ayurveda
35. Srimad Bhagavad Gita and Upanishad Connection
36. Srimad Bhagavad Gita - an attempt to summarize each chapter.
37. Facts and Impact of Nakshatra
38. Astro Gems - NAVARATNA
39. Ekadashi - A Concise Overview
40. A Concise View of Hanuman Chalisa
41. Inspirational Gita
42. Nakshatraranyam
43. Summary of 18 Mahapuranas
44. Synopsis of 18 Upa Puranas
45. Rigvediya Upanishads
46. Shukla Yajurvediya Upanishads
47. Krishna Yajurvediya Upanishads
48. Samavediya Upanishads
49. Atharvavediya Upanishads
50. The Seven Great Sages
51. From Rocket Scientist to President Dr. APJ Abdul Kalam
52. The Visionary's Voice - Quotes of Dr. APJ Abdul Kalam
53. The Wisdom of Swami Vivekananda: Insights and Inspiration from a Legendary Spiritual Teacher
54. Ayurvedic Remedies from the Garden
55. Sages and Seers
56. Rising Strong – Motivational Stories of Women
57. Beyond Flames -Mystery stories of Funeral Ghat Manikarnika
58. The Origins of Tulsi: A Look at the Mythological Roots of the Plant"

59. The Holistic Cow: A Look at the Physical, Spiritual, and Cultural Importance of Cows in India
60. Arts of Healing
61. Exploring the Divine
62. Understanding Five Elements
63. The Etymology of Ram
64. Symbols of India
65. Voice of Change (About Speeches of Great Men)
66. She Speaks (About Speeches of Great Women)
67. Patriotism on Celluloid – Brief About Patriotic Films
68. The Music of Motivation: A Brief Guide to Inspirational Film Songs
69. Unlocking the Secrets of the Dashopanishads
70. A Cultural Mosaic
71. Ancient Traditions, Modern Minds
72. Ecos of Ancient Wisdom
73. Beneath the Surface
74. From Temples to Ashrams
75. Sages of the Subcontinent
76. The Art of Healling (Ayurveda, Yoga & Naturopathy)
77. Indian Kitchen
78. The Festivals of India
79. The Indian Epics Retold
80. The Power of Mantras
81. The Indian River Ganges
82. The Indian Architecture
83. Rites of Passage
84. The Indian Silk Road
85. The Indian Literature
86. The Indian Villages
87. The Indian Folks & Crafts
88. The Way of Buddha
89. The Ramayan of Tulsidas

90. Astrological Remedies
91. The Secret Power of Motivation
92. Secret of Developing your Inner Strength
93. The Secret Path to Motivation
94. The Art and Secret of Positive Thinking
95. The Secrets of Practicing Ethical Living
96. Indian Art and Painting
97. The Indian Herbalism
98. Bharatanatyam to Kathak
99. Exploring India's Astrological Remedies
100. The Indian Festival of Flowers
101. Indian Handicrafts
102. The Splashes of Joy – India's Colour Festival
103. The Indian Science of Astrology
104. The Indian Mythology
105. Path to Enlightenment
106. The Indian Spirituality for Children
107. Aromas of India
108. The Secrets of Healthy Relationships
109. Ancestral Ties
110. The Indian Street Food
111. Discovering America
112. The Indian Textile
113. Listening to Motivational Speeches
114. Taste of India
115. A Cultural Journey through Indian Nuptials
116. Motivational Quote for Change
117. Secret Strategies for Making Money
118. Secrets to Cultivate a Positive Mindset
119. A Tapestry of Cultures: Exploring India from Kashmir to Kanyakumari
120. Achieving Your Dreams with Resilience: Secret Strategies for Overcoming Obstacles

121. Innovative Startups - 25 Startup Ideas to Spark Your Business Creativity
122. Export Management: Strategies for Global Success
123. Exporting from India - A Step by Step Guide
124. Finance Fundamentals: Mastering Financial Management for Business Success
125. Global Growth Strategies for International Business Development
126. Marketing Mastery: Unlocking the Secrets of Modern Marketing
127. Operations Mastery: Managing the Flow of Value in Business
128. Strategic Business Management: Navigating the Modern Business Landscape
129. Human Resource Management Strategies for Building and Managing a High Performance Team
130. The Indian Landscapes and Nature: An Exploration Of India's Natural Beauty And Diversity
131. The Indian Street Performances: A Cultural Exploration of India's Street Performances
132. Affirming Your Self-Worth: Strategies for Achieving Emotional Wellbeing
133. Cultivating Self-Discipline: Secrets Methods for Achieving Your Goals
134. Embracing Change: Strategies for Adapting to Life's Challenges
135. Embracing Your Uniqueness: Secret Strategies for Living an Authentic Life
136. Finding Motivation in Despondency: Coping with Difficult Times
137. Embracing Change
138. Learning to Love Yourself
139. Managing Time for Yourself

140. Unlock the keys to Self-Motivation
141. Secret to Boost Confidence
142. Unlocking your Potential: A Path to Inner-strength & Success
143. Secrets to Develop Authentic Relationship
144. Secrets to Build a Successful Career
145. Secrets to Live with Gratitude
146. Secrets to Create a Life of Abundance
147. Secrets to Cultivate Self-Awareness
148. The Power of Helping Hands
149. Finding Your Passion
150. The Indian Mythical Creatures
151. The Indian Women Saints
152. The Wisdom of the Saints
153. "The Indian Royalty: A Cultural and Historical Exploration of India's Maharajas and their kingdom"
154. The Mystic Land: A Cultural and Spiritual Exploration of India"
155. India's Spiritual Legacy – Discovering the Cultural and Religious Significance of Bhakti Yoga.
156. The Indian Folktales: An Exploration of India's Oral Folklore Traditions
157. Steeping In History: A Look at India's Iconic Tea Culture
158. The Indian Way Of Life: An Exploration Of The Philosophy And Practices Of Indian Culture
159. From Silence to Sound: A Cultural and Historical Study of Indian Cinema
160. Chronicles of Indian Style: Tracing the Transformations of Traditional and Contemporary Fashion
161. Decorating India: A Journey Through the Traditions and Transformations of Home Design
162. Adornments of India: A Journey Through the History and Artistry Behind Indian Jewelry

163. The Indian Royal Kitchens: A Gastronomic Journey Through the Kitchens of India's Maharajas
164. The Indian Sports: An Insight into the History and Significance of Indian Traditional Sports
165. "The Indian Traditional Games: A Study Of The Significance And Evolution Of Indian Traditional Games"

Contact

DR. JAGADEESH PILLAI

MBA & PhD in Vedic Science

Four Times Guinness World Record Holder

Winner of Mahatma Gandhi Vishwa Shanti Puraskar and
Global Peace Ambassador

Gemology, Astro & Vastu Consultant - Spiritual Counselor

Consultant for designing World Record Ideas

Efficient Tarot Card Reader

9839093003

myrichindia@gmail.com

drjagadeeshpillai@facebook

drjagadeeshpillai@instagram
jagadeeshpillai@youtube

www. JAGADEESHPILLAI.com

|| LOKAHA SAMASTHAHA SUKHINO BHAVANTU ||

9 798889 595670

Printed by Libri Plureos GmbH in Hamburg, Germany